GUATEMALA

GROLIER
EDUCATIONAL

Published 1999 by Grolier Educational
Sherman Turnpike, Danbury, Connecticut.
Copyright © 1999 Times Editions Pte Ltd. Singapore.

Set ISBN: 0-7172-9324-6
Volume ISBN: 0-7172-9332-7

CIP information available from the Library of Congress or the publisher

Brown Partworks Ltd.

Series Editor: Tessa Paul
Series Designer: Joyce Mason
Crafts devised and created by Susan Moxley
Music arrangements by Harry Boteler
Photographs by Bruce Mackie
Subeditor: Roz Fischel
Production: Alex Mackenzie
Stylists: Joyce Mason and Tessa Paul

For this volume:
Designer: Barbara Borup
Writer: Anita Dalal
Consultant: Berta Villamandos, Embassy of Guatemala, London.
Editorial Assistants: Hannah Beardon and Paul Thompson

Printed in Italy

Adult supervision advised for all crafts and recipes,
particularly those involving sharp instruments and heat.

CONTENTS

GUATEMALA:

Guatemala is part of the narrow land bridge that joins North and South America. With its neighbors, Belize and southern Mexico, it was home to the great ancient civilization of the Mayas.

▶**The Palacio Nacional** in the capital, Guatemala City, was built in the 1930s. It used to house all state offices but is to become a museum of the country's history. It has two Arabic-style courtyards, a two-ton gold and crystal chandelier, and frescoed inner walls.

First Impressions

- **Population** 10,322,000
- **Largest city** Guatemala City with a population of 1,132,730
- **Longest river** Motagua
- **Highest mountain** Tajumulco at 13,845 ft.
- **Exports** Cotton, sugar, beef, minerals
- **Capital city** Guatemala City
- **Political status** Republic
- **Climate** Tropical
- **Art and culture** Ruins of ancient Mayan civilization. Brightly colored textiles. An Important novelist is Miguel Angel Asturias.

▶**The churches of** Guatemala show the devotion of the Christian community. Most people are Roman Catholics, and the interiors of religious buildings are filled with beautiful statues and frescoes, or wall paintings. Their Christian faith sometimes shows elements of the early Native Indian beliefs of the people, but generally, the people hold strong Christian ideals.

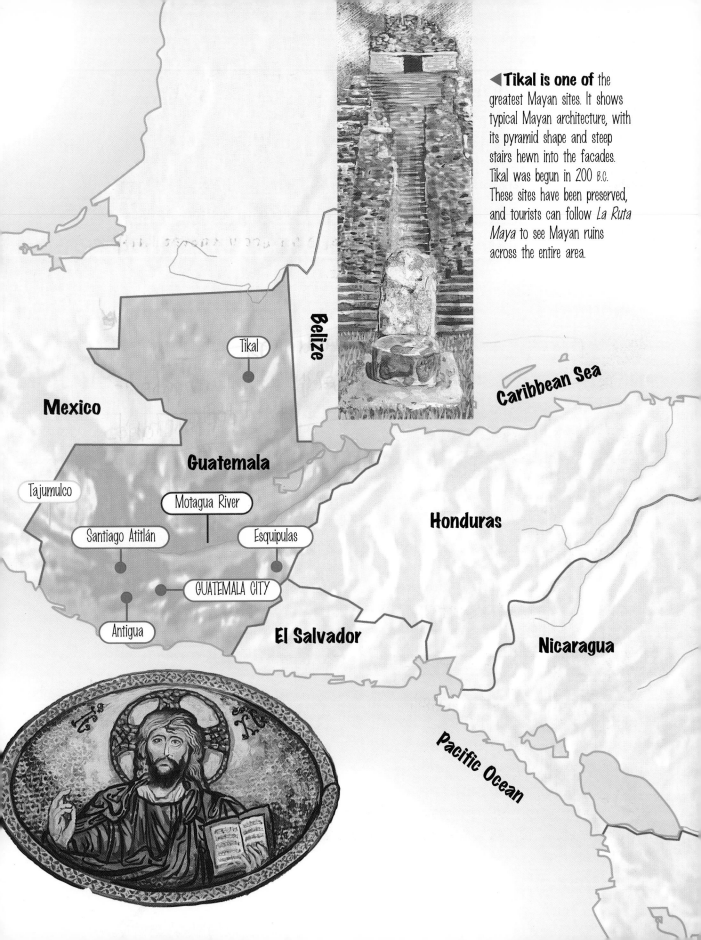

◄ Tikal is one of the greatest Mayan sites. It shows typical Mayan architecture, with its pyramid shape and steep stairs hewn into the facades. Tikal was begun in 200 B.C. These sites have been preserved, and tourists can follow *La Ruta Maya* to see Mayan ruins across the entire area.

Belize

Tikal

Mexico

Caribbean Sea

Guatemala

Tajumulco

Motagua River

Santiago Atitlán

Esquipulas

GUATEMALA CITY

Honduras

Antigua

El Salvador

Nicaragua

Pacific Ocean

RELIGIONS

For centuries the Mayan Indians worshipped their own gods.
When Spain conquered Guatemala 500 years ago, the Mayans became
Christians. The Indians, however, mixed old gods with the new faith,
and Mayan statues can be seen outside Christian churches.

GUATEMALA is a Christian country. Most of its people are Roman Catholics, and a few are Protestants. But in Guatemala the Christian faith is followed a little differently than in other countries.

Half of the people who live in Guatemala today are Indians. Their ancestors were the ancient Mayans, who ruled Guatemala a thousand years ago. The Mayan Indians worshipped many different gods and even offered human sacrifices to them at special fiestas.

In 1523 Spanish soldiers known as *conquistadors* invaded and conquered Guatemala. The Spanish were Roman Catholics. They built many churches in their colony, and their priests tried to make the Indians convert to Catholicism. But the Indians still believed in their own religion. They saw that many of the Catholic ceremonies were similar to their own, so they made a new religion that had bits of both faiths.

Today every village has a Catholic church. The Indians pray to the Christian god inside the church, but they also pray to their traditional gods on the steps outside the church. In the Indian villages there is both a Catholic priest and a shaman, the Mayan priest, and both are very important people.

The Protestant faith, another type of Christianity, is also becoming more and more popular in Guatemala. Missionaries, people who work to convert others to their religion, have converted many Guatemalans to Protestant Christianity. Even in small villages there is now often both a Catholic and a Protestant church.

GREETINGS FROM **GUATEMALA!**

Guatemala was conquered by Spain in the sixteenth century. The colonists brought their language with them, and now Spanish is the official language of the country. It is used by the government, the newspapers, by TV stations, and in schools. Half the people in Guatemala are descendants of Mayan Indians who married Spanish soldiers. They are called *ladinos,* and they speak only Spanish. But the other half of the population are direct descendants of the ancient Mayans. They still speak their own languages as well as Spanish and often wear traditional clothes.

Mayan languages are old and difficult to understand. In Guatemala there are 21 different Mayan languages. But the languages are so different from each other that if some Indians want to talk to each other, they have to speak in Spanish!

How do you say...

Hello

¡Hola!

How are you?

¿Como está?

My name is ...

Me llamo ...

Goodbye

Adiós

Thank you

Gracias

Peace

La paz

SANTIAGO ATITLÁN

*The people of Santiago Atitlán celebrate the feast day of **Santiago**, or Saint James, on July 25. They also worship a fierce god called Maximón.*

Saint James is an important saint in Guatemala. The Spanish introduced him to this country when they conquered it in the 1500s. They also brought horses here for the first time, so Guatemalans often have pictures of the saint riding a horse. He can be a destructive saint, so the people try not to upset him.

On July 25 each year the people of Santiago Atitlán, a pretty village by a big lake, have a fiesta to celebrate the saint's day. There is a big procession with fireworks and music. There is lots to eat and drink. Everyone wants the corn in the fields to grow, so they pray to Saint James to protect the crop.

This is an exciting and busy time in Santiago Atitlán, as the villagers also worship a very fierce god called Maximón. A week after Saint James's feast day the statue of

Every Sunday people come to worship Maximón. Bright scarves drape his neck, and cards surround him. He always wears a trilby hat. He is splashed with rum, and money is put in his lap. Women sit around smoking fat cigars, while others light candles to ask Maximón to keep their children safe from harm.

Maximón is moved to the home of a family selected each year for this honor.

This is a strange ceremony, but then Maximón is a strange god. He dresses in smart black clothes. He wears a trilby hat, and has scarves wrapped round his neck. He also smokes a giant cigar and wears dark glasses! He looks a very modern kind of deity.

The worshippers of Maximón bring him gifts of cigars and of rum. They also put playing cards on the table in front of him. People pray to Maximón to help them solve their problems or if they are sick.

It is a great honor to be asked to take care of Maximón for the year. A special group of villagers, known as the *cofradia,* selects a home. Every family has a room in which to keep the statue. This is decorated with flashing lights and plastic dolls. When the statue of Maximón is moved to his new home, the village has a great fiesta. The people in the village wear their best clothes.

Women wear a special hat made of a long ribbon that they coil around their head to make the shape of a flat saucer.

SAINT JAMES AND THE MOORS

This is the story of how the Spanish drove the Moors out of Spain and converted other countries to Christianity with the help of Saint James.

LONG AGO in Jerusalem a holy man called James preached a new faith called Christianity. James performed many miracles, but King Herod was frightened of him and had him executed. James's followers took his body to the coast, where a boat miraculously appeared and carried him to Galicia in Spain. He was buried in a field, which became known as the city of Santiago de Compostela.

Eight hundred years later Spain was conquered by the Moors, an Arab people who followed Islam. But the Spanish were Christians and wanted the Moors to leave their country. One day the Moors sent a message to the Spanish king Ramiro I, demanding that he send them 100 virgins as a tribute. Ramiro refused. The Moors became very angry and told him that they would collect the virgins by force. Ramiro mustered his small army of soldiers and waited for the Moors at Clavijo, near Najera.

On the first day of battle Ramiro's army lost many men. That night, as Ramiro prayed, a miraculous vision of Saint James appeared. It said he would help the Christians beat the Moors.

"But how?" pleaded Ramiro. "I have so few troops and they are all tired." But Saint James told him how to position his troops to win. Next day King Ramiro told his soldiers of

defeated, and Christianity was restored to Spain.

When the Spanish army went to South America in the sixteenth century to spread the holy word, a vision of Saint James resting on clouds traveled above the Spanish galleons. With the saint's help the Spanish converted Guatemala and other South American countries to Christianity, and the feast day of Saint James is celebrated on July 25 to mark the day Guatemala City, the capital of the country, was founded by the Spanish.

the vision, and with hearts lifted they charged into battle shouting: "Saint James, close in Spain!"

Suddenly Saint James descended from the sky on a great white horse. In one hand he carried a white shield with a red cross on it and in the other hand he carried a flashing sword. Saint James attacked the Moors so ferociously that he killed 60,000 of them. The army of Abderraman II was

CHRISTMAS

Christmas is celebrated on December 25 in Guatemala, just as it is all over the Christian world. It is a very important day, and everybody gives and receives gifts.

I n late December all the people of Guatemala look forward to the Christmas vacation, especially the children, who get lots of gifts. They decorate fir trees and send each other Christmas cards. This is the style of those living in towns or cities. However, the Indians who live out in the country have a very different way of celebrating Christmas.

All Guatemalans, whether they live in the city or in a village, know the important part of this festivity is the story of the Nativity – the story of the birth of Baby Jesus.

For most country people the story begins on December 16 with the *posada*, or

At Christmas families make a Nativity scene. It shows the stable at Bethlehem where Jesus was born. Little figures of Jesus, Mary, Joseph, and the Three Wise Men are added to it. These scenes are often big and brightly painted. They are made out of clay, cardboard, or metal.

"shelter." Every night until Christmas Eve families carry figures of Mary and Joseph from house to house. They knock on neighbors' doors asking for a place for the images to spend the night. This ritual recalls how long it took Mary and Joseph to find a place to stay.

The Mary and Joseph figures are moved every night until Christmas Eve. Then, at last, they can rest in one house until the day of January 6. They take their place in the creche — the model of the stable where Jesus was born.

Now the Christmas celebrations can start. Everybody enjoys some snacks and a hot punch drink. The family goes to church to attend the Midnight Mass held on Christmas Eve. After the Mass everyone lets off fireworks.

Most people go home to a special meal of *tamales*, a flat dough, doughnuts with honey sauce, and fresh fruit. The children are given presents on Christmas Day. In some homes the gifts are left under the tree, but in others the children find their gifts under their pillows.

13

SEMANA SANTA

In Guatemala Holy Week, or Easter, is called **Semana Santa.** *It is the biggest and most colorful fiesta in Guatemala. Antigua has the best festival. It is a time for planting, and Indians also ask their gods to give them a good harvest.*

Semana Santa is a time of solemn celebration here. All the stores close, and there are long religious rituals and processions. Easter falls in the growing season, so the Indian people, who are farmers, also pray to their old gods for a good harvest.

The grandest of Holy Week processions happens in Antigua. This city was the capital of Guatemala when the country was ruled from Spain. People travel from far and wide to be part of the Easter program in Antigua.

Just before Good Friday local people make big stencils of birds, flowers, and religious symbols. They lay them down on the streets and sprinkle them with

During Easter women carry floats with figures of the Virgin Mary covered in red roses. There are many shrines to Mary. She is honored as the mother of Jesus.

NO-COOK SALSA

SERVES SIX
4 tomatoes
1" piece of cucumber
4 scallions
2 limes
1 green capsicum
Fresh coriander leaves
Salt and pepper
Corn chips to serve

Halve, quarter, then chop the tomatoes finely. Chop the cucumber and scallions finely. Place the chopped ingredients in a bowl. Squeeze the juice from the limes and add to the mixture.

Remove the stems and stalks from the coriander leaves and chop finely. Set aside a couple of leaves for decoration. De-seed the capsicum and chop finely. Add the coriander and capsicum to the bowl. Mix thoroughly. Season to taste with salt and pepper. Serve with corn chips.

colored saw-dust. When the stencils are removed, the street is beautifully decorated.

The celebrations begin early on Good Friday. Riders, dressed as Roman soldiers, call for the death sentence on Jesus. Floats carry the figures of the Virgin and Saint John.

The most special float of all carries the effigy of Jesus. The men who pull this float are allowed to walk on the stencilled shapes on the street. All others must walk on the sides. These men in charge of Christ wear purple clothes until 3 p.m. on Good Friday, the time Jesus died on the cross. Then they put on black clothes until Easter Sunday to show they mourn the death of Jesus. Easter Sunday is a day of joy celebrated with music and dance.

On Good Friday people gather at the city hall. They sing the "Song of Pardon" to forgive those who crucified Christ. Then a prisoner is set free.

15

CORN FESTIVAL

*Corn is the most important food in Guatemala.
The gods are asked to look after the corn when
it is planted. At harvest they are thanked for the crop.*

In the Indian villages corn is part of every meal. Both *tortillas* and *tamales* are made of it. Indians also have a sweet drink called *horchata*, made from cornmeal and cinnamon. People even feed corn to their animals. The villagers use corn stalks to make roofs for their houses. The early Guatemalans believed that humans were first created from corn. Because corn is so very important, there are age-old rituals to mark both the planting and the harvest. These festivals used to be held everywhere, but today only a handful of villages celebrate them.

The planting time for corn is from March to May. When they decide the time is best for planting, all in the

The Guatemalans love to wear brightly colored traditional clothes, especially at fiesta time. They often weave special patterns of birds, animals, plants, and saints into the cloth to ensure good luck. The tortoise below is an incense burner. Most people are farmers, and motifs from nature are often seen in their art and crafts.

village help to prepare the land, clearing the soil so that the seeds can be sown. The first or second Sunday before planting people take the corn seeds to church. The seeds are blessed in a special Mass. Families light

candles, burn incense, and scatter flower petals around the corn seed. Everybody kneels in a circle to pray for a good harvest. They sometimes dye ears of corn red, yellow, white, and blue and make pretty mosaics from them that are laid out on the church floor.

Everybody tries to be good in the weeks before planting. They do not want to offend the gods. The night before planting men sprinkle alcohol on the fields and burn incense. On the day of planting everybody comes out to the field to watch. They bring food and candles, that are placed either at the four corners of the compass or in the way of the wind.

When the planters have finished, everyone has a feast in the fields.

The corn is harvested in the winter. Whole families work together to gather it. They play music as they work. When the harvest is ready, the corn is carried back to the village in a procession. There is music, dancing, and fireworks are let off. The harvest meal is a feast of turkey and good local fruit.

Make a Felt Appliqué Wallhanging

The Guatemalans love to make brightly colored wallhangings. The beautiful designs celebrate their ancient Mayan myths.

YOU WILL NEED

13" long bamboo stick
12" x 20" piece of
plain, light-colored felt
Brightly colored felts for the pattern
2 x 15" lengths of colored wools
Glue
Scissors

Wallhangings are a traditional craft in Guatemala. They are intricate hand-woven designs that often tell a story. You can make your own wallhanging using felt shapes.

1 Draw your designs on paper. Then cut out the shapes and draw around them on felt. Cut out the felt shapes and glue onto the large piece of felt.

2 Cut out two rectangles of felt 3" long and 2" wide. Make a fringe on each by snipping along their length. Leave ½" at the end of each.

3 Glue along the ½" strip of one fringe and wrap around one end of the stick. Braid the colored wools together and tie one end around the tassel.

4 Glue along the top edge of the back of the wallhanging. Fold back and press down. Leave a gap for the bamboo stick.

5 Thread the bamboo stick through the gap and attach the other tassel as in step 3. Tie on the other end of the string.

HUNAB AND THE CORN MEN

This is the story of how Hunab, father of all the gods, created men out of corn to live in the world he had just created.

A LONG TIME AGO, before the world existed, there was nothing but darkness everywhere. Then the great god Hunab, the father of all the other gods, created the world. He made 13 heavens in the sky, which he arranged layer on layer. The lowest layer became the Earth. Then he made 13 levels of the underworld beneath the Earth. The lowest one was ruled by the god of death.

Hunab wanted to create people who could live in his new world and look after the gods. To begin with he tried making them out of mud. He shaped them care-fully, but they just melted away. So Hunab destroyed the mud people in a flood and asked the other gods what he should do. The gods suggested that Hunab use harder material, so he made some new people out of wood.

The wood people were more successful than the mud people. They could move about but only on all fours like animals, and they could have children. But the wooden people had no souls or minds. They could not even remember who had created them. Hunab was furious, so he created another flood to get rid of them.

Next Hunab made men out of flesh and women out of reeds. But they would not even talk to him. Hunab was so angry he allowed them to be eaten by the other animals and birds.

Hunab tried one last time. This time he used corn. Four animals – a mountain cat, a coyote, a parrot, and a crow – brought him ears of corn. Hunab used the ears of corn to shape bodies. He made cornmeal dough and used it for the arms and legs. He then created four men: Mahucutan, Balam-Quitzé, Balam-Acab, and Iqui-Balam.

The corn men looked at the world and were very happy as there was lots of corn to eat. The corn men were also very wise and almost as perfect as the gods. This worried Hunab so he made them a little less intelligent. While the corn men slept, they each dreamed of a pretty wife, and when they woke up, their wives were real. The corn men and women became the fathers and mothers of the whole human race.

PATRON SAINTS

Roman Catholic Christians believe that their saints will help them by talking to God on their behalf. Many groups and villages have a special saint, a "patron saint," who looks after everybody in that community.

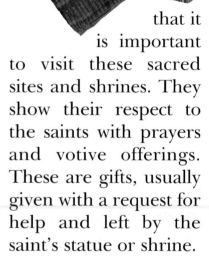

Guatemala has lots of fiestas every year to celebrate saints. Most villages have their own patron saint. On that saint's special day the schools close and no one goes to work.

Life in the villages is simple but hard. People weave their own clothes and grow their own food. Their saint helps them and deserves a party.

Some of these special festivals take place when people travel on pilgrimages, religious journeys to the shrines of saints. Most of the people here believe that it is important to visit these sacred sites and shrines. They show their respect to the saints with prayers and votive offerings. These are gifts, usually given with a request for help and left by the saint's statue or shrine.

One of the biggest pilgrimages happens on January 15 each year. People visit a town called Esquipulas. Here there is a statue called the Black Christ. The statue got its name because it is made from a very dark wood that has been made black over hundreds of years

A LA RORRO NINO

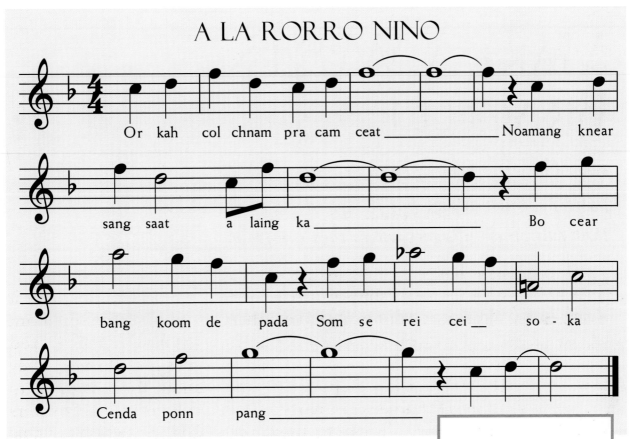

Or kah col chnam pra cam ceat _____ Noamang knear

sang saat a laing ka _____ Bo cear

bang koom de pada Som se rei cei __ so - ka

Cenda ponn pang _____

A Lullaby
Lullaby my baby,
Lulla lullaby,
Go to sleep my baby,
Go to sleep my love.

by candle smoke and incense. The statue is five feet high, dressed in white satin, stitched in gold thread, and covered in jewels.

When the pilgrims arrive at the church, they often approach the statue on their knees because they have so much respect for it. In the countryside the villages' saint's days are celebrated with music and noisy fireworks.

MAKE A WOVEN BRACELET

Woven bracelets are made in brightly colored patterns. Each village has its own design that tells other villagers where they are from.

These bracelets are given as a sign of friendship. They can be made in many colors, so every single one is different. Why not make two the same and give one to a special friend so that you can share it?

YOU WILL NEED
8 x 32" strands of white thread
1 x 28" thin stick
¼" wide strips of fabric
Some different colored wools
A large needle
1 ice-cream stick and scissors

1 Take the eight strands of white thread and tie them together in a simple knot at one end. Repeat at the other end. Now tie one end to the end of the stick. Tie the other end of the threads to the other end of the stick, pulling it into a bow. This is makes the loom. The threads form the warp.

2 Take the ice-cream stick and weave it through the threads, one up, one down, at one end of the loom. With the fabric strip weave a few rows at the other end of the loom.

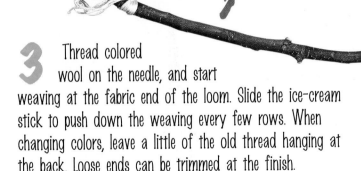

3 Thread colored wool on the needle, and start weaving at the fabric end of the loom. Slide the ice-cream stick to push down the weaving every few rows. When changing colors, leave a little of the old thread hanging at the back. Loose ends can be trimmed at the finish.

4 When you have completed the weaving, cut one end from the loom and tie the eight warp threads together in pairs. Do the same at the other end.

5 Braid the warp threads and tie the ends. Cut any loose ends from the back of the weaving.

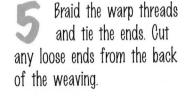

NEW YEAR

In Guatemala the New Year is a time for dancing, eating, and drinking and for letting off fire-crackers. Some Indians also celebrate the Mayan New Year and pray to ancient gods.

Most people in Guatemala celebrate New Year on January 1. Everybody celebrates at home with their families. They dance, let off fireworks, and have special food and drink.

But some Indians in Guatemala celebrate New Year twice. This is because they use two calendars. One is the regular Christian calendar of 365 days. The other is an old calendar invented by their ancestors, the Mayans, which tells them when to celebrate festivals.

Momostenango is one of the biggest towns in Guatemala. Its people still celebrate all the festivals of the old Mayan calendar. This calendar is very different from ours. It has 18 months, not 12, and each month has just 20 days. The last month has only five days. Though the Mayan year has 365 days like ours, the

BROKEN POTTERY

The Guatemalan Indians believe that if a plate or cup breaks, it is because the gods want it to happen, and so the pieces really belong to the gods.

On New Year's Day the villagers go to traditional outdoor altars and make offerings of broken pottery. Then they pray for good luck for the coming year.

Mayan New Year is celebrated every 260 days, so Mayan New Year's Day is on a different day each year.

The New Year is marked by a huge fiesta in Momostenango. On the final day of the old year the Indians go to church to light candles and say prayers.

The next day, at daybreak, they walk to their ancient traditional altars. These big outdoor mounds are about half a mile from the church. The Indians burn incense and pray. When it gets dark, the celebrations begin.

In the churches the priests pray for two days. The shamans, the guardians of the old Mayan beliefs, chant at their altars. The people celebrate with food and drink bought from special festive stalls. They let off fireworks to welcome the New Year.

The puma has a special place in the legends of Guatemala. Its strength, speed, and secrecy are admired. Masks imitating other animals or mythical beasts are worn at the secret Mayan ceremonies of New Year. Food is simple but good. A corn pancake contains meat and beans.

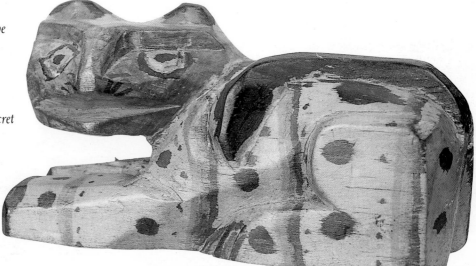

TODOS SANTOS

One day a year the ancestors return to Earth. Their families celebrate this with a ritual at the cemetery. They gather at the graves with flowers and food and await the arrival of the dead.

The people of Guatemala celebrate All Saints' Day, also called *Todos Santos*, on November 1. It is a public holiday, so all the workplaces are shut for the day. Most people pack food and flowers, and spend the day at the cemetery.

The Guatemalans believe that their dead ancestors return to Earth every year on this day. It is important to give them a very good welcome. Yellow is the color of death in Guatemala and the living make decorations of yellow flowers. These are hung in doorways at home. Families gather at the graves, and all help to clean and tidy them. Crosses of yellow flowers are placed on the graves. It is not a sad time, because the Guatemalans believe that their ancestors are all together now.

The families and friends also bring food so that their dead relatives will not be hungry when they return to Earth. A favorite food

made for the dead relatives is a salad called *fiambre*. It includes a bit of everything: sausage, chicken, meat, fish, some vegetables, hard-boiled eggs, cheese and spices.

The Indians also make a jam from pumpkin and black sugar. The jam is left at the head of the grave. This food is called *cabecrea*, or "head piece."

There is a picnic atmosphere in the cemeteries. Old friends greet each other, families catch up on gossip, and the children play. Next day the food left for the dead is gone.

In the village of Santiago Sacatepequez there is a particular custom. Food and flowers are brought for the dead, as everywhere else, but in this village they also bring kites to the graves. These are made of wood and colored paper. All the children are given small kites, and in the evening everyone flies their kites from the graves of their ancestors. The sky is full of bright, cheerful colors that greet the dead. Yellow crosses make the Earth welcoming for returning ancestors!

CHICKEN IN PINEAPPLE

Put the chicken pieces in a heavy casserole. Add all the other ingredients. Stir to mix well. Cover the casserole and simmer over a low heat for about 45 minutes or until the chicken is tender. Serve on a bed of rice.

SERVES SIX

3 lb chicken pieces
15 oz can pineapples in unsweetened fruit juice
2 onions, finely chopped
2 tomatoes, peeled and chopped
2 cloves garlic, finely chopped
2 whole cloves
1 t. cinnamon
½ cup white wine vinegar
½ cup olive oil
1 t. salt
½ t. pepper

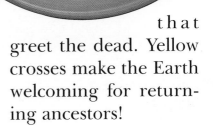

SAINT THOMAS

Every year the town of Chichicastenango celebrates the feast day of Saint Thomas, a disciple of Christ who saw Him rise up from the dead.

On December 21 the people of Chichicastenango cele-brate the feast day of Saint Thomas, or Santo Tomás. He is the Catholic patron saint of the town.

All week people gather outside the Catholic church to buy and sell goods at the market. There are many noisy, happy processions. On the last three days men jump off a 100-foot flying pole with a rope tied to one ankle and spin to the ground.

Inside the church lots of candles burn, and the floor is covered in pine needles and rose petals. On the feast day everyone joins the procession, and statues are carried in the town.

WORDS TO KNOW

Altar: A table on which worshippers leave offerings, burn incense, or perform ceremonies.

Feast Day: A day on which a religious event or the life of a saint is celebrated.

Incense: A mixture of gum and spice, shaped into thin sticks or cones, that makes a pleasant smell when burned.

Mass: A Christian ritual in which bread and wine are used to commemorate the Last Supper of Jesus Christ.

Mayans: The Indian people who lived in Guatemala before the arrival of the Spanish.

Missionary: A person who travels with the aim of converting others to his or her religion.

Moors: A Muslim people from northwest Africa who conquered Spain in the eighth century.

Muslim: A follower of the religion of Islam.

Patron saint: A saint who is special to a particular group. Nations, towns, and professions have patron saints.

Pilgrim: A person who makes a religious journey, or pilgrimage, to a holy place.

Protestant: A member of one of the Protestant churches, which together form one of the main branches of Christianity. The Protestants split from the Roman Catholic Church in the sixteenth century.

Relic: A part of the body, clothing, or belongings of Jesus or a saint, preserved as a holy item.

Roman Catholic: A member of the Roman Catholic Church, the largest branch of Christianity. The head of this church is the pope.

Sacrifice: To give up something that is greatly valued for an even more important reason.

Saint: A title given to very holy people by some Christian churches. Saints are important in the Roman Catholic Church.

Shamanistic: Followers of shamanistic religions believe in a hidden world of spirits who can be contacted by a priest or priestess known as a shaman.

ACKNOWLEDGMENTS

WITH THANKS TO:
Tumi South American Crafts, London. Vale Antiques, London. Embassy of Guatemala, London.

PHOTOGRAPHY:
All photographs by Bruce Mackie except: John Elliott pp. 15, 29. Marshall Cavendish p. 26. Cover photograph by Corbis/Dave G.Hauser.

ILLUSTRATIONS BY:
Fiona Saunders pp. 4 – 5. Tracy Rich p. 7. Robin Shadwell pp. 21, 29. Maps by John Woolford.

Recipes: Ellen Dupont.

Set Contents